D1625360

A Heart Full of Peace

A HEART
• FULL OF •
PEACE

Joseph Goldstein

WISDOM PUBLICATIONS • BOSTON

Wisdom Publications
199 Elm Street
Somerville MA 02144 USA
www.wisdompubs.org

Library of Congress
Cataloging-in-Publication Data
Goldstein, Joseph, 1944–
  A heart full of peace / Joseph Gold-
stein.—[New ed.].
    p. cm.
  Based on the Wit lectures given at the
Harvard Divinity School in 1993.
  Previously published: Transforming the
mind, healing the world. New York :
Paulist Press, c1994.
  ISBN 0-86171-542-X (hardcover : alk.
paper)
  1. Spiritual life—Buddhism. I. Gold-
stein, Joseph, 1944– Transforming the
mind, healing the world. II. Title.
  BQ5675.G657 2007
  294.3'444—dc22

                                2007015533

11 10 09 08 07
5 4 3 2 1

This book is based on the Wit Lectures
given at the Harvard Divinity School in
1993 and published at the time by Paulist
Press. In revising the manuscript for this
new edition, the author has drawn on other
writings, including an article in the Sham-
bhala Sun magazine.

Cover and interior design by
Gopa & Ted2, Inc. Set in Village 9.8/18.

Wisdom Publications' books are printed
on acid-free paper and meet the guidelines
for permanence and durability of the Production Guidelines for Book Longevity of
the Council on Library Resources.

Printed in the United States of America

This book was produced with
Environmental Mindfulness. We
have elected to print this title on 50%
PCW recycled paper. As a result, we have
saved the following resources: 23 trees, 16
million BTUs of energy, 2,060 lbs. of
greenhouse gases, 8,549 gallons of water,
and 1,098 lbs. of solid waste. For more
information, please visit our website,
www.wisdompubs.org

For Sarah

A truly gracious being,
with a heart full of peace.

Publisher's Acknowledgment

The publisher gratefully acknowledges the generous help of the Hershey Family Foundation in sponsoring the production of this book.

Contents

Foreword

IN THIS SMALL BOOK Joseph Goldstein conveys with clarity and concision some of the spiritual teachings, beliefs, values, and practices we urgently need to help balance the materialism of our age—compassion, love, kindness, restraint, a skillful mind, and a peaceful heart. Joseph originally presented this teaching as part of Harvard Divinity School's Wit Lectures on Living a Spiritual Life in the Contemporary Age. He reveals the need to combine faith with practice, freedom with responsibility, and action with contemplation. I, too, am firmly of the opinion that those who sincerely practice Buddha Dharma must also serve society. Too often we make what we call "the happiness of all beings" the object of our prayers and meditations, yet when we rise from our meditation cushions we fail to give practical help to our neighbors and others in need. If we are to fulfill our altruistic wish, we cannot discriminate between spirituality and our life in society. Without the support of our fellow beings we could not practice at all, and without a concern for their welfare our practice has little meaning.

Tenzin Gyatso
The Dalai Lama

· A Heart Full of Peace ·

LOVE, COMPASSION, AND PEACE—
these words are at the heart of spiritual
endeavors. Although we intuitively resonate
with their meaning and value, for most of us,
the challenge is how to embody what we
know: how to transform these words into a
vibrant, life practice. In these times of conflict
and uncertainty, this is not an abstract exercise. Peace in the world begins with us. In the
following pages, we will explore different
ways we can manifest these values as wise and
skillful action in the world.

These teachings are based on the Buddhist

traditions of the East, but their defining characteristic is not Eastern or Western, but rather, an allegiance to pragmatism and the very simple question: "What works?" What works to free the mind from suffering? What works to engender the heart of compassion? What works to awaken us from ignorance?

**In the cherry blossom's shade,
there's no such thing
as a stranger.**

ISSA

This pragmatism also illuminates an age-old question that continues to plague religious and other traditions: how can we hold strong differences of view in a larger context of unity, beyond discord and hostility? The answer is of vital importance, especially now, as we see the grand sweep of religious traditions often in vio-lent conflict with one another.

Love, compassion, and peace do not belong to any religion or tradition. They are qualities in each one of us, qualities of our hearts and minds.

MAY ALL BEINGS BE HAPPY

The Sanskrit word *maitri* and the Pali word *metta* both mean "loving-kindness" or "loving care," and refer to an attitude of friendliness, good will, and generosity of heart. When we are filled with loving-kindness and a sense of loving care, we have a very simple wish: May all beings be happy.

This kind of love has many qualities that

distinguish it from our more usual experiences of love mixed with desire or attachment. Born of great generosity, metta is a caring and kindness that does not seek self-benefit. It does not look for anything in return or by way of exchange: "I will love you if you love me," or "I will love you if you behave a certain way." Because loving-kindness is never associated with anything harmful, it always arises from a purity of heart.

One of the unique aspects of metta is that it does not make distinctions among beings. When we feel love mixed with desire, this feeling is always for a limited number of people. We may love and desire one person, or maybe two or three at a time, or maybe several in series. But does anyone in this world *desire* all beings?

I make my mind my friend.

JAPANESE SAMURAI POEM

Loving-kindness, on the other hand, is extraordinary precisely because it can embrace all; there is no one who falls outside of its domain. That is why, when we encounter people who have developed this capacity to a great extent—the Dalai Lama, for example—we sense their tremendous kindness toward everyone. Loving-kindness is a feeling that blesses others and oneself with the simple wish, "Be happy." The Japanese poet Issa expresses this openhearted feeling so well: "In the cherry blossom's shade, there's no such thing as a stranger."

Although we may not always live in a steady

state of loving feeling, through practice we can learn to touch it many times a day.

THE PRACTICE OF LOVING-KINDNESS FOR ONESELF

One way to develop and strengthen metta within us is through the following specific meditation practice, which we start by extending loving feelings toward ourselves.

It's very simple: At first, just sit in some comfortable position, and keeping an image or felt sense of yourself in mind, slowly repeat phrases of loving-kindness for yourself: *May I be happy, may I be peaceful, may I be free of suffering.* Say these or any other phrases that reflect feelings of care and well-wishing, over and over again. We do this not as an affirmation, but rather as an expression of a caring *intention.* As you repeat the words, focus the mind on this intention of kindness; it slowly grows into a powerful force in our lives.

Although the practice is straightforward, at times it can be extremely difficult. As you turn your attention inward and send loving wishes toward yourself, you might see a considerable amount of self-judgment or feelings of unworthiness. At these times, proceed gently, as if you were holding a young child. A line from an old Japanese Samurai poem expresses well this part of the practice: "I make my mind my friend."

THE PRACTICE OF LOVING-KINDNESS FOR A BENEFACTOR

After strengthening feelings of loving-kindness for ourselves, we then send these very same wishes to a benefactor, someone who has aided us in some way in our lives. This might be a parent, a teacher, or even someone we don't know personally, but whose life has nonetheless had a positive influence on our own. One person who was having difficulty connecting with loving-kindness said that she opened to the feeling of metta most easily when she thought of her dog—a being who always gave her unquestioning love. Benefactors can take many forms.

In this part of the practice, hold the image or sense of that person (or other being) in your mind, as if you were talking directly to them, and then direct your intention of metta toward him or her: *Be happy, be peaceful, be free of suffering.*

This stage is often easier than directing metta toward ourselves, because we usually already have warm and caring feelings for those who have helped us.

THE PRACTICE OF
LOVING-KINDNESS FOR ALL

From a benefactor, we move on to other cate-gories of people. We send loving wishes to loved ones who are very close to us personally; then to those who are neutral, about whom we have no strong feelings one way or another; and then to "enemies" or difficult people. Finally, we send loving-kindness to all beings everywhere.

It's important to move through this progres-sion at your own speed. There is no timetable. Some categories may be easier than others. Whenever you feel that you're able to generate genuine feelings of loving-care for one, move on to the next.

This can be practiced intensively in the soli-
tude of a meditation retreat, in our daily practice at home, or even as we're walking down the
street or driving to work. In all cases, it begins
to change how we relate to others in the world.

**May you be happy, may you be peaceful,
may you be free from suffering.**

As an experiment, the next time you are
doing an errand, stuck in traffic, or standing on
line at the supermarket, instead of being preoc-
cupied with where you're going or what needs
to be done, take a moment to simply send loving wishes to all those around you. Often, there
is an immediate and very remarkable shift

inside as we feel more connected and more present.

When I first began the practice of metta, I had an experience that revealed a lot about my mind and the way I was relating to others. At the time, I was developing loving-kindness toward a neutral person—although I wasn't really sure what a "neutral person" meant. My teacher, Anagarika Munindra, simply said to pick someone nearby for whom I didn't have much feeling, one way or another.

I was in India at the time, and there was an old gardener at the little monastery where I was staying. I saw him every day, but I had never really given him any thought at all. He was just somebody I noticed in passing. It was quite startling to realize how many such people there

were around me, beings for whom I had completely neutral feelings. That in itself was an
illuminating discovery.

So every day for weeks, I began visualizing
this old gardener in my meditation, repeating
phrases like "May you be happy, may you be
peaceful, may you be free from suffering." After
a while, I began to feel great warmth and caring for him, and every time we passed my heart
just opened.

This was a great turning point in my practice. I understood that how I feel about someone is up to me, and that my feelings do not
ultimately depend on the person, his or her
behavior, or the situation. The gardener re-
mained the same. He did not change what he
was doing or how he related to me. But
because of a turn in my own understanding

and practice, my heart began to fill with genuine feelings of kindness and care.

WHAT LEADS
TO TRIUMPH OF HEART?

There is an important lesson here about the sustaining power of loving-kindness. Because it does not depend on any particular quality in the other person, this kind of love does not transform easily into ill will, anger, or irritation, as love with desire or attachment so often does. Such unconditional love—love literally without conditions—comes only from our own generosity of heart.

Although we may recognize the purity and power of this feeling, we may fear or imagine that this kind of love lies beyond our capacity. But metta is not a power that belongs only to the Dalai Lama or Mother Teresa or some extraordinary being categorically different from ourselves. We can all practice this power within ourselves and actually learn to love in this way. The question for us is *how* can we do it? What makes this inclusiveness possible?

A number of years ago, the *Harvard Medical Journal* included an article about a Tibetan doctor named Tenzin Chodak, who had been a personal physician to the Dalai Lama. In 1959, Dr. Chodak was imprisoned by the Chinese for twenty-one years. For seventeen of those twenty-one years, he was beaten and tortured daily—physically and psychologically—and his life was continually threatened. Astonishingly, he emerged from this twenty-one-year-long horror virtually free from signs of any kind of post-traumatic stress.

In the article, Dr. Chodak distills the wisdom we need to understand into four points of understanding, which made possible not only his survival—people survive horrendous conditions in many ways—but also the great triumph of his heart. A short biographical sketch of him by Claude Levenson describes him in this way: "An appearance almost of timidity on first meeting, a voice so quiet it might be a whisper... Dr. Chodak could easily pass unnoticed, until you meet his gaze—a gaze filled with the perception of one who has seen so much that he has seen everything, seeing beyond the suffering he has experienced, beyond all the evil and the abuses he has witnessed, yet expressing boundless compassion for his fellow human beings."

FOUR INSIGHTS IN
TIMES OF DISTRESS

We must endeavor to see every situation in a larger context. Like the Dalai Lama—who often speaks of how one's enemy teaches one patience—Dr. Chodak saw his enemy as his spiritual teacher, who led him to the wisest and and most compassionate place in himself. Accordingly, he felt that even in the most dreadful and deplorable circumstances some human greatness, some greatness of heart, could be accomplished. Of course, thinking this is easy; the challenge is to remember and apply this understanding in times of difficulty.

Second, we must see our enemies, or the difficult people in our lives, as human beings like ourselves. Dr. Chodak never forgot the commonality of the human condition. The Eastern "law of karma" means that all our actions have consequences: actions bear fruit based on the intentions behind them. People who act cruelly toward us are actually in adverse circumstances, just as we are, creating unwholesome karma that will bring about their own future suffering.

But we mustn't fall into thinking of karma as, "They'll get theirs," as a kind of vehicle for cosmic revenge. Rather, seeing the universal human condition can become a wellspring of compassion. The Dalai Lama said, "Your enemies may disagree with you, may be harming you, but in another aspect, they are still human beings like you. They also have the right not to suffer and to find happiness. If your empathy can extend out like that, it is unbiased, genuine compassion." Understanding karma—that we all reap the fruit of our actions—as a vehicle for compassion is the wisdom we could now integrate into our lives. We're all in the same situation with regard to the great law of karmic cause and effect.

Third, we must let go of pride and feelings of self-importance. These attitudes, which can arise so easily in times of conflict, become the seeds of even more difficulty. It doesn't mean that we should adopt a stance of false humility or self-abnegation. Rather, we let go of the tendency toward self-aggrandizement, whether interpersonally or within the framework of our own inner psychology. A story from ancient China uses nature to illustrate the great protection of true humility:

The sage, Chuang-Tzu, was walking with a disciple on a hilltop. They see

a crooked, ancient tree without a single straight branch. The disciple says
the tree is useless, nothing from it can
be used, and Chuang-Tzu replies,
"That's the reason it's ancient. Everyone seems to know how useful it is
to be useful. No one seems to know
how useful it is to be useless."

Dr. Chodak actually attributed his survival
to the ability to let go of *self-importance* and *self-
righteousness*. This insight provides a tremendous lesson on the spiritual journey, a lesson
that can come up for all of us again and again.

Finally, the insight that nourished Dr. Chodak's amazing triumph of the heart, and one
we must truly understand ourselves, is that
hatred *never* ceases through hatred; it ceases

only in response to love. Many spiritual traditions acknowledge this truth. In situations of
conflict, loving-kindness and compassion grow
when we understand them to be the most beneficial motivation for responsive and effective
action.

Hopefully, most of us will never be tortured
by our enemies; but can we hold these perspectives, even in less trying circumstances? When
someone is very angry with you or you're in
some difficult situation, remember that this difficulty, itself, can strengthen patience and love.
In these situations, we can investigate what
greatness of heart we might accomplish, remind
ourselves that everyone involved shares the
common bond of humanity, let go of pride, and
understand that, in the end, hatred and enmity
will only cease by love.

**If my mind doesn't go out
to disturb the noise,
the noise won't disturb me.**

AJAHN CHAH

Years ago I was practicing meditation in India and facing a circumstance that, at the time, felt quite challenging to my inner peace and well-being. The summer months had grown very hot on the Indian plains, and I decided to continue my meditation in a rented cottage in the mountains. Situated at seven thousand feet, the hill station of Dalhousie has spectacular views of the high Himalayan peaks. It was beautiful and quiet, and I settled into a routine of silent, intensive practice.

Just below my cottage was a big, open field,

and a few weeks after I arrived, a group called the Delhi Girls pitched their tents. The Delhi Girls were a kind of paramilitary Girl Scout troop. Not only did they set up camp, they also set up loudspeakers, blaring loud Hindi film music from six o'clock in the morning until ten o'clock at night.

I watched my mind go through a tremendous range of emotions, from real frustration and anger, to an outraged feeling of self-importance —"How can they do this to me? I came all the way to India to get enlightened!"

It took quite a while for my mind to work through all that, to let go of the feelings of self-importance and self-righteousness and *just let things be.* As Ajahn Chah, a great Thai meditation master of the last century, once said of a noisy celebration near his meditation hut: "If my mind doesn't go out to disturb the noise, the noise won't disturb me." There in the mountains of India, when my mind finally did settle down, the continual din of film music in the middle of a meditation retreat was no longer a problem.

OPENING TO COMPASSION

In Buddhist practice, we develop awareness of the different motivations that underlie our actions. We also open to the possibility of expanding our highest motivation and aspira- tions. This actually enlarges our sense of what we can accomplish in our lives.

**Our highest motivation
enlarges our sense
of what we can accomplish.**

Bodhichitta is a Sanskrit and Pali word that literally means "the awakened heart." This refers
to that deep wish to awaken from the dream of
ignorance in order to benefit all beings.
Through cultivating this aspiration, we dedicate
our spiritual practice and our very lives to the
happiness and welfare of all.

But is this aspiration realistic? Is it really possible to cultivate such an altruistic motivation,
given the great mix of qualities within our
minds?

Even His Holiness the Dalai Lama has said,
"I cannot pretend I always practice bodhichitta,

but it does give me tremendous inspiration. Deep inside me I realize how valuable and beneficial it is. That is all." If we, too, can realize how valuable and beneficial it is, we can simply *plant the seed* of bodhichitta in our minds, and trust that it will slowly take root and grow in our lives. Repeated short moments of bodhichitta are powerful imprints in our minds. Just as a small seed can become a giant redwood, these moments of bodhichitta are the seeds for many wholesome actions. As the great naturalist, Henry David Thoreau, wrote, "Convince me that you have a seed there and I am prepared to expect wonders." We might begin each day or each period of meditation with whatever resolve expresses our deepest wish, finding the words that most inspire us. For example, we might say, "May I quickly attain liberation for the welfare and happiness of all beings." Doing this regularly leads us from the understanding that our spiritual practice inevitably helps others, simply by becoming kinder and more peaceful ourselves, to making the benefit of others the very motivation for our practice.

This shift in understanding transforms the way we move through the day—with a generous heart, a heart that wishes well to all beings rather than just a few, a heart full of peace. With such a heart, whenever we come close to suffering in the world, we are moved to help alleviate it. That *impulse to act* is compassion.

**Oh that my monk's robes
were wide enough to gather up
all the people in this floating world.**

RYOKAN

The willingness to come close to suffering opens us to compassionate action. We don't have to look far to find suffering. The nightly news programs are catalogs of the world's distress. Are we open to it? Do we actually relate to what we see and hear, or has it all become too de-personalized?

The Japanese hermit-monk Ryokan, who created such wonderful poetry, wrote: "Oh that my monk's robes were wide enough to gather up all the people in this floating world."

Are we indeed open to the suffering of "all

the people in this world"? Are we even open to the suffering in our own bodies and minds? It is the nature of the body to become sick, to fall ill, and to feel pain as well as pleasure. Such things don't always wait for old age; they can happen at any time. Sometimes we feel this painful aspect of experience is a mistake, forgetting that it's part of the natural order of things. It is simply the way things are.

Certain emotions and mind-states also create suffering in our lives: anger, hatred, fear, loneliness, anxiety, boredom, greed, and many others. Even if we have a fair degree of material comfort, a sense of unease or dissatisfaction often colors our inner world.

Sometimes we feel the painful aspect of experience is a mistake.

Opening to suffering is the doorway to compassion; but many times we find we're not open.
We've been strongly conditioned to avoid or
defend ourselves against pain: "Let me not see
any suffering. Let me not feel it."

Avoidance becomes obvious in meditation
when we experience some physical discomfort.
People coming to meditation for the first time
often think, "I'll go on a wonderful retreat and
spend a few days in bliss." But meditation is
not about just feeling good; it is about coming
in touch with whatever is actually present.

Especially at the beginning of the practice,

most of us get in touch with some physical pain. And then there are our various reactions to it: fear, self-pity, defensiveness, or avoidance. Mostly, we just don't like it. We try to just "watch the pain" but really we are trying to bargain with it: "I'll watch you... if you go away."

All of these responses are quite different from opening to discomfort, allowing it, and simply feeling it with bare attention.

Our relationship to unpleasant physical sensations in meditation reveals a lot about our relationship to pain in other life circumstances. In similar ways, we close off to emotions that make us uncomfortable, feelings of anger, sadness, fear, unworthiness, and so on. Think of all the ways we try not to feel bored: all the busyness and distractions we create. Or reflect on the great lengths to which we go out of our fear of feeling lonely. Unwilling to be with this unpleasant feeling or explore it within us, we often build whole structures in our lives to avoid feeling it.

If this fear is here for the rest of my life, it's okay.

A transforming moment of my meditation practice came when I was lost for several days in recurring feelings of intense fear. I tried being aware of them as they arose, noting "fear, fear." But I still felt caught in the intensity of the emotion. Then, at a certain point, something shifted in my mind, and I said to myself, "If this fear is here for the rest of my life, it's okay." That

was the first moment of genuine acceptance—
and it entirely changed my relationship to fear.
Fear would still arise, of course, but I no longer
locked it in with my resistance. Genuine mindful acceptance allowed the fear to just wash
through.

It's not always easy to be compassionate,
much as we want to or even feel that we are.
We don't like opening to our own pain, and
we don't necessarily want to open to the pain
of others. It takes practice—and perhaps several different practices—to be able to open to
the difficult emotions that we're aware of and
to illuminate those that are hidden. But with
mindfulness, our hearts become spacious
enough to hold painful emotions, to feel them,
and to let them go. And the more mindful and
aware we become of our own physical or

emotional difficulties, the more strength, courage, and insight we have in being with the suffering of others.

Compassion is a verb.

THICH NHAT HANH

With the aspiration of bodhichitta—the wish for our lives to benefit all—something power-ful begins to happen. At first, we feel a genuine empathy for others in pain or difficulty. This happens when we take a moment to stop and feel what's really going on, before rushing on with our lives. We then move from empathy, which is a sympathetic feeling for others, to compassion—which is more than simply a warm feeling.

Compassion contains a strong motivation to *act*. The Vietnamese monk, Thich Nhat Hanh, expressed this so well in saying, "Compassion is a verb."

True compassion means actively engaging with the suffering in the world, and responding to the various needs of beings in whatever ways are possible, whatever ways are appropriate.

At times, compassion might take the form of small, perhaps unregarded, acts of being just a little kinder, more generous, or more forgiving of the people around us. At other times, it might require acts of tremendous courage and determination in the face of hardship and difficulty. There is no particular prescription for what to do. The field of compassionate response is limitless: it is the field of suffering beings. The important thing is to water and nurture the seed of bodhichitta within us and cultivate the intention to benefit all.

Where there is hatred, let me sow love.

SAINT FRANCIS OF ASSISI

Six weeks after 9/11, I was teaching loving-kindness meditation at a retreat for lawyers. We began by sending loving wishes to ourselves, and then to the various categories of beings. At the retreat, I suggested the possibility of including in our metta even those involved in acts of violence and aggression. One of the participants from New York commented that he couldn't possibly send loving-kindness to al-Qaeda, nor would he ever want to.

For me, that simple and honest statement raised a lot of interesting questions. What is our response to violence and injustice? How do we understand the practices of loving-kindness and compassion in the face of fear or anger? What are our bedrock aspirations for the world and ourselves?

In doing the meditation on loving-kindness, we repeat the phrases "May you be happy, may you be peaceful, may you be free of suffering." However, when we get to people who have done us harm, either individually or collectively, often we don't want to include them in our loving wishes. We don't *want* to wish them happiness. We may well want to see them suffer for the great harm they have done. These are not unusual feelings to have. But right there, in that situation, is the critical juncture of contemplative practice and action in the world.

**May everyone be free of hatred,
free of enmity.**

If we want to enhance the possibilities for more compassion and peace in the world—and in ourselves—we need to look beneath our usual emotional responses. In situations of suffering, whether small interpersonal conflicts or huge disasters of violence and destruction, one question holds the key to a compassionate response: In this situation of suffering, whatever it may be, what is our most fundamental wish?

In the current Middle East situation, with so much violence on all sides, I find my metta practice including all in this wish: "May you be free of hatred, may you be free of enmity."

If our aspiration is peace in the world, who would we exclude from this wish? Terrorists, suicide bombers, soldiers lost in violence, government policy-makers? "May everyone be free of hatred, free of enmity." If our own response to the mind states that drive harmful acts is more enmity, hatred, or ill will, we are part of the problem—whether we acknowledge it or not.

This message is not new, but the challenging question remains: What to do with these feelings when they arise because, for almost all of us, they will. And how do we find compassion in the midst of storms of anger, hatred, ill will, or fear?

**Suffering is nothing but experience
enslaved to ignorance.**

THE DALAI LAMA

Most importantly, we need to acknowledge
the feelings that arise. In this regard, it's mindfulness that brings the gift of compassion—for
others and ourselves. Mindfulness sees the
whole parade of feelings, however intense,
without getting lost in them, and without judging ourselves for feeling them.

Much of the time, we live in denial. It's not
easy to open to our shadow side. Our habitual reaction to most unpleasant or painful
experiences is to avoid them. And even when
we are aware of our feelings of hatred and
enmity, we may get caught in justifying them

to ourselves: "I *should* hate these people, look at what they did."

Justifying feelings is quite different than being mindful of them. From justifying comes a strong feeling of self-righteousness. We forget that our feelings and emotions are all conditioned responses, arising from our own perspective, from the particular conditions of our lives; someone else in the same situation might feel very differently. We often forget that our feelings don't necessarily reflect some ultimate truth. Self-righteousness about our feelings and views is the shadow side of commitment. We may confuse self-justification with feelings of passionate dedication. But great exemplars of compassion and social justice—people like Martin Luther King, Jr., Gandhi, Aung San Suu Kyi, and others—illuminate the difference.

It is not a question of *whether* but *when* un-wholesome mind states will arise in us or the world around us. Feelings of hatred, enmity, fear, self-righteousness, greed, envy, and jeal-ousy will all arise. The challenge is to see them all with mindfulness. See that they cause suf-fering and that no action based on them will lead to our desired result: peace within and peace in the world.

Ordinary situations in our lives can fre-quently provoke a deeper awareness. Walking down a city street, for example, we may pass by homeless people. It's really a dreadful situ-ation that in a country as prosperous as ours so many people live on the streets. For me, it's illuminating to watch my mind as I walk by.

Watching the moon at dawn,

solitary, mid-sky,

I knew myself completely.

No part left out.

IZUMI

What do you do, personally, as you pass
them by? Are you aware of the way you relate
to these fellow human beings? Do you really
register that this is the situation, this is the suffering, occurring right now? Or, because it is
too unpleasant, too distressing, do you close
yourself off?

Someone once asked Dr. Paul Farmer, the
great humanitarian health worker in Haiti
and other countries around the world, why
he would spend all day walking to a remote

village to care for just a few people. His reply revealed the universal, boundless capacity of compassionate action:

"If you say that seven hours walk is too long to walk for two families of patients, you're saying that their lives matter less than some others. And the idea that some lives matter less is the root of all that's wrong with the world."

The practice of compassion means letting experience in. Another Japanese poet, a woman named Izumi, who lived in the tenth century, wrote: "Watching the moon at dawn, solitary, mid-sky, I knew myself completely. No part left out." When we can open to all parts of ourselves and to others in the world, something quite extraordinary happens. We begin to connect with one another.

**The idea that some lives
matter less is the root of all
that's wrong with the world.**

PAUL FARMER

One of the most memorable experiences in
my meditation practice occurred quite a few
years ago. I was doing a Zen sesshin—an intensive meditation retreat—with Joshu Sasaki
Roshi, a very fierce old Zen master. Roshi
worked with the koan method. A koan can be
a question the master gives you that does not
have a rational answer. One of the most famous
koans is "What is the sound of one hand clap-
ping?" The idea is to penetrate the essential
meaning, and then to demonstrate your understanding in your response to the teacher.

In this sesshin, we all met with Roshi four times a day to give him the answer to our koan. Everything in the sesshin is very structured, building the tension and the charge in the mind. I would go in with my answers, but often Roshi would just say, "Oh, very stupid," and then ring his bell to dismiss me. Once I gave my answer and he said, "Okay, but not Zen." With each interview I was getting more and more uptight.

Finally, he had a little compassion for me and gave me an easier koan. He asked, "How do you manifest the Buddha while chanting a sutra?" A sutra is a Buddhist text and we had been doing some chanting of sutras every day. Well, I thought I finally understood the koan: I would simply go in and chant a little of the sutra.

**To receive compassion and love,
one must be willing to open
to one's vulnerability.**

I don't think Sasaki Roshi knew it at the time, but this koan touched some deep conditioning within me. It went back to my third grade singing teacher, whose advice to me was "Just mouth the words." From then on, I had a strong inhibition about singing in public—yet here I was, having to perform in the pressure cooker of a sesshin.

Sesshin is held in silence except for inter-views and chanting, and everything in the mind becomes hugely magnified. I was a total wreck. I rehearsed two lines of the sutra over and over, all the while getting more and more tense.

When the bell rang for the interview, I went in, did my bows, started chanting—and completely messed up. I got all the words wrong, and the simple melody was non-existent. I felt completely exposed, vulnerable, and raw.

In that moment, something quite special happened. Roshi looked at me, and with uncharacteristic tenderness said, "Oh... very good." It was a moment of heart touching heart, still vivid after many years. In this powerful moment I saw that to receive compassion and love one must be willing to open to one's vulnerability. Then we can connect heart to heart.

CLEAR SKY, OPEN MIND

What is the wisdom that gives rise to compassion? What do we need to understand in order to stay open to suffering?

Genuine happiness does not come from accumulating pleasant feelings.

It is a realization both simple and profound: genuine happiness does not come from accumulating more and more pleasant feelings. When we reflect on our lives and the many nice things and pleasant feelings we've experienced, have they provided us with lasting fulfillment? We know that they have not—precisely because they don't last.

Society and popular culture reinforce our belief that happiness comes primarily through pleasant feelings. One advertisement for cigarettes pictures a beautiful man and woman lounging together in a paradisiacal setting, holding cigarettes in their hands. The caption reads, "Nothing stands in the way of my pleasure." We may have seen through this with regard to smoking, but the principle still looms large in our lives: Get this and you'll be happy, feel that and you'll be happy.

The tremendous danger is that this belief— that genuine happiness comes only from pleasant feelings—becomes a strong motivation to stay closed to anything unpleasant. But by staying closed to all unpleasantness, we also stay closed to our own wellspring of compassion.

There is no higher happiness than peace.

THE BUDDHA

The transforming realization of meditative awareness is that happiness does not depend on pleasant feelings. But if that is the case, where does true happiness come from? This is the question at the heart of meditation practice.

Meditation is the art of true relationship. Whenever there is sorrow or joy, anger or love, fear or courage, there are also many possible ways to relate to these emotions. Do we get caught in them? Do we identify with them? Is the mind spacious and accepting, or do we get lost in judgment?

We might think of the mind as being like clear, open space. All kinds of things can arise there, but the space itself is not affected. It is possible to develop a mind like that, a mind not lost in or attached to phenomena. Such a mind experiences a much more abiding kind of happiness, because it doesn't depend on changing conditions. After experiencing the rush of pleasant experience so many times, at a certain point, we realize the wisdom of the Buddha's statement, "There is no higher happiness than peace." We actually have moments when we know this to be true.

In meditation and in our lives, it is not so important what particular experience arises. What's important is how we relate to it. By learning to relate well with whatever arises, we open to the full range of human experience, to what the Taoists call "the ten thousand joys and the ten thousand sorrows." This deepening of understanding and wisdom fosters the growth of compassion within us.

THE PRACTICE OF COMPASSION

It is important to see compassion as a practice. Sometimes we may feel it, sometimes not. At times, the suffering we encounter may seem too much and we may need to back off, close off a little, to prevent being overwhelmed. At such times, we need to create a space where we can regain our strength and balance. From a place of renewed strength, we can then open up once again. As with loving-kindness, the more we practice compassion, the stronger it becomes in our lives.

> **Try to be at peace with yourself and help others to share that peace.**
>
> THE DALAI LAMA

There is no hierarchy of compassionate action. Based on our interests, skills, and what truly moves us, we each find our own way, helping to alleviate suffering in whatever way we can. If we let in all the parts of ourselves and our world, the whole world becomes a field for compassionate action.

The Dalai Lama goes to the heart of things in the most simple and down-to-earth way. "We are visitors on this planet," he has said. "We are here for ninety, one hundred years at most. During that period we must try to do something good, something useful with our lives. Try to be at peace with yourself and help others to share that peace. If you contribute to other people's happiness, you will find the true goal, the true meaning in life."

It is very simple. We are here for a very short time. Can we try to do something good with our lives? Can we develop an inner peace and share that inner peace with others? When we contribute to other people's happiness, we find the true meaning and true goal of life. This is our task. This is our challenge.

· The Practice of Freedom ·

A CENTRAL QUESTION confronting spiritual life today is how to best respond to the tremendous conflicts and uncertainties of these times. The seemingly intractable violence of the Middle East, poverty and disease, racism, degradation of the environment, and the problems in our own personal lives all call us to ask: What is the source of this great mass of suffering? What forces in the world drive intolerance, violence, and injustice? Do we really understand the nature of fear and hatred, envy and greed? And are there forces that hold the promise of peace? Do we know how to cultivate love and kindness, energy and wisdom?

TRAINING THE HEART

The great discovery of the meditative journey is that all the world's forces for good and for harm are also playing out right here in our own minds. If we want to understand the world, we need to understand ourselves.

The Buddha taught that three fields of training are the essence of spiritual practice. First, in the field of morality, we train to pay attention to our actions and speech, and to realize that everything we do and say has consequences. We cannot divorce spiritual practice from the everyday actions of our lives. The foundation of morality is the principle of not harming: not harming others, not harming ourselves.

Given this understanding, it's intriguing that in our society the word *morality* can sometimes have negative connotations. People may confuse it with self-righteousness or being *moralistic*. While these associations may make us shy away from the term, the refinement of non-harming is essential for the spiritual path.

THE PRACTICE OF TRAINING IN MORALITY

To embody our commitment to morality, we need to pay attention to what we do, waking up to our actions of body, speech, and mind. How do we train ourselves to do this? We can begin by watching the effect an action has on our minds. When we do something, how does it affect us? How do we feel? What qualities does this particular action strengthen?

Every time we get angry, we practice anger. Every time we're filled with resentment, we are practicing resentment. The more these mind states are present and acted upon, the stronger they become. Every time we feel loving or perform some kind, generous act, this is what we strengthen. Each and every action is our practice, because some quality of heart and mind is actually being developed.

Try not to become a person of success. Rather become a person of value.

ALBERT EINSTEIN

We can practice paying attention in the midst of very ordinary activities. When you talk with people, do you know what's happening in your mind? When you eat or work, do you know what qualities are being strengthened? Pay attention, also, to how your actions affect others, staying sensitive to the effect of your energy on them. We are often so caught up in our own stories or perspectives, we don't see the impact we're having.

Training in morality, or non-harming, means developing a greater sensitivity to those around us, and taking care with the effect our actions might have.

One demanding and far-reaching arena of practice is becoming aware of the *motives* behind our speech and actions. This is very subtle, and there is tremendous room here for self-delusion. We may think we're acting with great purity; yet when we look honestly and deeply, we may see otherwise.

Here is a simple example from my time practicing meditation in Asia: Anybody who
spends time in India must come to terms with
the many beggars on the streets. It's an
unavoidable part of reality there. One day, as
I was in the bazaar buying some fruit, there
was a little boy standing next to the stall holding his hand out. He looked hungry, and so I
gave him one of the oranges I had just bought.
It wasn't really a big thing at all, just a simple,
spontaneous act.

Then something happened that was very
revealing. The boy took the orange and just
walked away: not a smile, not a thank-you, not
even a nod of the head. Nothing. Only then, in
the absence of any kind of engaging response,
did I see clearly that some part of my mind and
my motivation wanted acknowledgment. Of

course, I had not expected effusive thanks for an orange—but I saw I had expected something.

The only thing I can rely on is my sincere motivation.

THE DALAI LAMA

The influence of different motives on our minds is very subtle. Part of training in morality is becoming more honest with ourselves. It takes tremendous awareness, even courage, to look at ourselves with this kind of interest and openness.

But how do we practice this training in morality? So often when we hear teachings we say, "Yes, that's a good idea. It's good not to harm." We may even coast on a sense of being basically moral people—because, after all, we aren't people who go around killing, stealing, or doing other obviously harmful things. But the real awakening comes when we see that we can greatly *refine* our morality. Wherever we are in our lives and whatever our commitment is to doing no harm, our moral sense can be expanded, perhaps taking us beyond our current comfort zone. One teacher expressed it this way: if one is truly committed to living in accord with the precepts of nonharming, there should be some discomfort. This is what makes the practice of morality so powerful and life changing.

Religious traditions express their basic moral precepts in many different ways, but they also have much in common. In traditional

Buddhism, laypeople practice five precepts: not killing, not stealing, not committing sexual misconduct, not using wrong speech, and not taking intoxicants that confuse the mind. These basic guidelines are very simple, and are understood not as commandments but as rules of training. Each of these precepts is a practice in itself.

Be happy—or call the exterminator?

Some time ago I was getting a haircut in a barbershop. A fly was buzzing around, and the barber grabbed his fly swatter and killed it. From an ordinary worldly perspective, killing a fly is nothing; people do it all the time. But from the moral perspective of non-harming, we don't need to go around killing flies or other insects we find annoying. Would it be possible to catch it in a cup and place it outside, saving life, rather than destroying it? By changing our relationship to other living creatures, we connect with the life that is within even those small beings.

This is not to suggest the answers are always clear-cut. Sometimes there are strong competing values at play. If termites or carpenter ants are slowly eating up your house, what do you do? Do you simply say, "Be happy," do you find a way to encourage them to leave, or do you call the exterminator? Ethical decisions are not always easy. But if we're committed to looking for alternatives to killing, we can take the practice of nonharming further than we might already have.

In whatever we do, it's important that we look at our own mind-states. Are we practicing ill-will and aversion or are we cultivating compassion and wisdom? And even in situations when we are doing something harmful, if we know it's unskillful, even as we're doing it, that is already the beginning of wisdom. That awareness can become the seed of future change.

THE PRACTICE OF MINDFULNESS OF SPEECH

We can also practice morality in speech, which is a huge area of activity in our lives. Speech is a powerful force that conditions our own minds and strongly affects those around us. But how much attention do we pay to our speech: to what's behind it, what motivates it, what really needs to be said? Often, we are so caught up in our own thoughts, ideas, and feelings, the words simply tumble out.

By making right speech an active part of our spiritual path, we can bring wisdom and sensitivity to what we say.

When I was first learning about Buddhism and right speech, I conducted a little experiment. For several months I decided not to speak about any third person. I'd not speak about anyone to someone else; in other words, no gossip, even of a harmless kind. Surprisingly, a very large percentage of my speech was eliminated.

This experiment had a significant impact on my mind. I noticed that much of my speech was some kind of comment or judgment about others. By completely stopping such speech for a while, my mind became less critical—not only of others, but also of myself.

> **Wanting great insights without a grounding in moral action is like putting tremendous effort into rowing across a river, without untying the boat from the dock.**
>
> ANAGARIKA MUNINDRA

Although I'm not quite as rigorous now, by making right speech a practice, I find that a little inner warning bell still goes off if I'm about to say something about others. This awareness offers the opportunity to bring some discernment to the intention, and often I simply let the thought go. This is a very simple example of the gift of renunciation: we don't have to give voice to every passing thought in our minds. Surprisingly, rather than being a burden or hardship, this restraint creates a feeling of ease and well-being.

These are things that have significant impact in our lives: impact on how we live and how we feel. This is what morality is about. It is not something abstract. It is something we train ourselves in: not killing or stealing, not committing sexual misconduct, not engaging in wrong speech, or taking intoxicants that make us heedless. These precepts are important guidelines, especially in our society where many traditional values are no longer in place.

We need to take care with our actions. Passion and desire are powerful and seductive forces. When they are present in the mind, we may often feel most alive. But under their influence, we sometimes do things that are unskillful, and rationalize behaviors that cause harm to ourselves and others. "Crimes of pas-sion" fill the newspapers and are staples of popular fiction—and although our own actions may not make the headlines, we can still see some of these tendencies at work in ourselves.

The writer Anne Lamott, with truth-striking humor, described how difficult it is to deal with the triumphs of other writers, particularly if one of them happens to be a friend: "It can wreak just the tiniest bit of havoc with your self-esteem to find that you are hoping for small, bad things to happen to this friend, for, say, her head to blow up."

And desire is so often glamorized in adver-
tising and media, it's as if increasing one's
desire is something to aim for. One advertisement even co-opted a spiritual message in its
effort to foster more wanting. The picture
shows a man in front of some new car, which
itself was surrounded by all of the techno-
gadgets that one would ever want. The caption read, "To be one with everything, you *need*
one of everything."

The practice of morality is the foundation
of a spiritual life. When one of my first teachers visited America, he met many people who
were interested in meditation, but not so committed to the practice of moral training. He
commented that wanting great meditative
insights without a grounding in moral action
is like putting tremendous effort into rowing

across a river, without untying the boat from the dock.

We can put tremendous effort into many kinds of meditative techniques, but if we are not committed to the basic foundation of non-harming, we will not actually progress in the spiritual life.

> **Our practice is not to follow the heart;**
> **it is to train the heart.**
>
> AJAHN SUMEDHO

Ajahn Sumedho is a wonderful American monk now living in England, who trained for many years with the great Thai meditation master, Ajahn Chah. With great succinctness,

Ajahn Sumedho said: "Our practice is not to follow the heart; it is to train the heart." This is a tremendously important distinction.

Often we hear the adage, "Follow your heart." But having practiced and looked at all the things that have arisen in my heart, I've seen that while some things were fine and beautiful, many were not so noble. The heart is not only driven by love, kindness, and compassion; it is also driven by desire, greed, and anger. We need to train the heart, not simply follow it.

The commitment to morality, or non-harming, is a source of tremendous strength, because it helps free the mind from the remorse of having done unwholesome actions. Freedom from remorse leads to happiness. Happiness leads to concentration. Concentration brings wisdom.

And wisdom is the source of peace and freedom in our lives.

The refinement of a moral life is also one of the causes for dying without confusion: living a moral life helps us to die with a clear mind. And one of the most beautiful aspects of nonharming is the great gift of fearlessness, which we bestow on everyone we meet. When we commit to non-harming, we are saying through our actions, "There is no cause for fear." This gift of trust is a very precious gift to the world.

Everything flowers, from within,
of self-blessing.

GALWAY KINNELL

We have all acted unskillfully at times. But the strength and power of morality is renewed the moment we re-commit ourselves to skillful action. Not that we'll always be totally pure; that's unrealistic. But we do need to understand that this training is the foundation of wise living.

Imagine life on this planet if we followed just part of the precept not to kill: by simply not killing other people, the world would be transformed into a very different place. If we are committed to awakening, it's essential to train our hearts in this way.

The Buddha taught that morality—not physical appearance or outer adornments—is the true beauty of a human being. We all recognize this, when we're with people who live from that place of basic goodness within. By refining our own practice of morality, or non-harming, we relearn our loveliness.

As New England poet Galway Kinnell wrote in "Saint Francis and the Sow":

> The bud
> stands for all things,
> even for those things that don't flower,
> for everything flowers, from within,
>   of self-blessing;
> though sometimes it is necessary
> to reteach a thing its loveliness,
> to put a hand on its brow
> of the flower
> and retell it in words and in touch
> it is lovely
> until it flowers from within, of self-
>   blessing.

CONCENTRATING THE MIND

The practice of morality, non-harming, is the first field of training. The second field of training has to do with the development of concentration and a strong, mindful awareness.

Mindfulness is the key to the present moment. Without it we cannot see the world clearly, and we simply stay lost in the wanderings of our minds. Tulku Urgyen, a great Tibetan Dzogchen master of the last century, said, "There is one thing we always need, and that is the watchman named mindfulness—the guard who is always on the lookout for when we get carried away by mindlessness."

Mindfulness is the quality and power of mind that is deeply aware of what's happening—without commentary and without interference. It is like a mirror that simply reflects whatever comes before it. It serves us in the humblest ways, keeping us connected to brushing our teeth or having a cup of tea.

> **There is one thing we always need, and that is the watchman named mindfulness.**
>
> TULKU URGYEN

Mindfulness also keeps us connected to the people around us, so we don't just rush by them in the busyness of our lives. The Dalai Lama is an example of someone who beautifully embodies this quality of caring attention. After one conference in Arizona, His Holiness requested that all the employees of the hotel gather in the lobby, so that he could greet each one of them before he left for his next engagement.

Mindfulness is the basis for wise action. When we see clearly what is happening in the moment, wisdom can direct our choices and actions, rather than old habits simply playing out our patterns of conditioning.

Why don't you start meditating?

And on the highest level, the Buddha spoke of mindfulness as the direct path to enlighten- ment: "This is the direct path for the purifica- tion of beings, for the overcoming of sorrow and lamentation, for the disappearing of pain and grief, for the attainment of the Way, for the realization of nirvana."

I began to practice meditation when I was in the Peace Corps in Thailand. At the time I was very enthusiastic about philosophical discussion. When I first went to visit Buddhist monks, I arrived with a copy of Spinoza's *Ethics* in my hand, thinking to engage them in debate. Then I started going to discussion groups for Westerners, held at one of the temples in Bangkok. I was so persistent in my questions that other people actually stopped coming to the groups. Finally, perhaps out of desperation, one of the monks said, "Why don't you start meditating?"

I didn't know anything about meditation at the time, and I became excited by the prospect of what I saw as an exotic Eastern practice. I gathered all the paraphernalia together, sat myself down on a cushion—and then set my alarm clock for five minutes. Surprisingly, something important happened even in those few minutes. For the first time, I realized there was a way to look inward: there was a path for exploring the nature of my mind.

This realization is a turning point in everyone's spiritual life. We reach a certain point in our lives when something connects, and we acknowledge to ourselves, "Yes, I can do this." All of this was so new and interesting to me that, for a while, I'd invite my friends over to watch me meditate. Of course, they didn't often come back.

THE PRACTICE
OF MINDFULNESS

We can start the practice of mindfulness meditation with the simple observation and feeling
of each breath. Breathing in, we know we're
breathing in; breathing out, we know we're
breathing out. It's very simple, but not easy.
After just a few breaths, we hop on trains of
association, getting lost in plans, memories,
judgments, and fantasies. Sometimes it seems
like we're in a movie theater where the film
changes every few minutes. Our minds are like
that. We wouldn't stay in a theater where the
movies changed so rapidly, but what can we do
about our own internal screening room?

This habit of wandering mind is very strong,
even when our reveries aren't pleasant and, perhaps, aren't even true. As Mark Twain so aptly

put it, "Some of the worst things in my life never happened." We need to train our minds, coming back again and again to the breath and simply beginning again.

**Some of the worst things
in my life never happened.**
MARK TWAIN

As our minds slowly steady, we begin to experience some inner calm and peace. From this place of greater stillness, we feel our bod-ies more directly and begin to open to both the pleasant and unpleasant sensations that might arise. At first, we may resist unpleasant feel-ings, but generally they don't last that long.

They are there for a while, we feel them, they're unpleasant—and then they're gone and something else comes along. And even if they come up repeatedly, over a period of time, we begin to see their impermanent, insubstantial nature and to be less afraid of feeling them.

A further part of the training is becoming aware of our thoughts and emotions, those pervasive mental activities that so condition our minds, our bodies, and our lives. Have you ever stopped to consider what a thought is—not the content but the very nature of thought itself? Few people really explore the question "What is a thought?" What is this phenomenon that occurs so many times a day, to which we pay so little attention?

Not being aware of the thoughts that arise in our mind, nor of the very nature of thought itself allow thoughts then dominate our lives. Telling us to do this, say that, go here, go there, thoughts often drive us like slaves.

Unnoticed,

thoughts have great power.

Once, when I was teaching in Boulder, Colorado, I was sitting quite comfortably in my apartment. Thoughts were coming and going, when one arose in my mind that said, "Oh, a pizza would be nice." I wasn't even particularly hungry, but this thought lifted me out of the chair, took me out the door, down the stairs, into the car, over to the pizza place, back into the car, up the stairs, and into my apartment, where I finally sat back down to eat the pizza. What drove that whole sequence of activity? Just a thought in my mind.

Obviously, there is nothing wrong with going out for pizza. What does merit our attention, though, is how much of our lives is driven by thoughts. Unnoticed, they have great power. But when we pay attention, when we observe thoughts as they arise and pass away, we begin to see their essentially empty nature. They arise as little energy bubbles in the mind, rather than as reified expressions of a self.

"Pay no attention to that man behind the curtain."

THE WIZARD OF OZ

Just as there was no all-powerful wizard behind the curtain in *The Wizard of Oz*, the only
power our thoughts have is the power we give
them. All thoughts come and go. We can learn
to be mindful of these thoughts and not be carried away by the wanderings of our mind. With
mindfulness, we can exercise wise discernment: "Yes, I will act on this one; no, I'll let that
one go."

In the same way, we can train ourselves to
be mindful of emotions, those powerful ener-
gies that sweep over our bodies and minds like
great breaking waves. We experience such a
wide range of emotions, sometimes within
quite a short period of time: anger, excitement,
sadness, grief, love, joy, compassion, jealousy,
delight, interest, boredom. There are beautiful
emotions and difficult ones—and for the most

part, we are caught up in their intensity and the stories that give rise to them.

WORKING WITH EMOTIONS

We easily become lost in our own melodramas. It's illuminating to drop down a level and look at the energy of the emotion itself. What is sadness? What is anger? Seeing more deeply requires looking not at the emotion's "story," but at how the emotion manifests in our minds and bodies. It means taking an active interest in discovering the very nature of emotion.

Ajahn Sumedho expressed this kind of interest and investigation very well. He suggested that in a moment of anger or happiness, we simply notice: "Anger is like this," "Happiness is like that." Approaching our emotional life in this way is quite different than drowning in the intensity of feelings or being caught on the rollercoaster of our ever-changing moods.

To do this takes mindfulness, attention, and concentration. We need to take care, though, not to misunderstand this practice and end up suppressing emotions or pushing them aside. The meditative process is one of complete openness to feelings. From the meditative perspective, the question is, "How am I relating to this emotion?" And completely identified with it or is the mind spacious enough to feel the grief, the rage, the joy, the love without being overwhelmed?

THE PRACTICE OF LETTING GO

As you meditate, keep bringing your attention back to what is happening in the moment: the

breath, a feeling in the body, a thought, an emotion, or even awareness itself. As we become
more mindful and accepting of what's going on,
we find—both in meditation and in our lives—
that we are less controlled by the forces of denial
or addiction, two forces that drive much of life.
In the meditative process we are more willing
to see whatever is there, to be with it but not
be caught by it. We are learning to let go.

Open the hand of thought.

KOSHO UCHIYAMA

In some Asian countries there is a very clever
trap for catching monkeys. A slot is made in
the bottom of a coconut, just big enough for

the monkey to slide its hand in, but not big enough for the hand to be withdrawn when it's clenched. Then they put something sweet in the coconut, attach it to a tree, and wait for the monkey to come along. When the monkey slides its hand in and grabs the food, it gets caught. What keeps the monkey trapped? It is only the force of desire and attachment. All the monkey has to do is let go of the sweet, open its hand, slip out, and go free—but only a rare monkey will do that. And similarly, the twentieth-century Japanese Zen teacher Kosho Uchiyama speaks of "opening the hand of thought."

Another quality that develops in meditation is a sense of humor about our minds, our lives, and our human predicament. Humor is essential on the spiritual path. If you do not have a sense of humor now, meditate for a while and it will come, because it's difficult to watch the mind steadily and systematically without learning to smile. Someone once asked Sasaki Roshi whether he ever went to the movies. "No," he replied. "I give interviews."

**Love your crooked neighbor
with all your crooked heart.**

W.H. AUDEN

Some years ago I was on retreat with the Burmese meditation master Sayadaw U Pandita. He is a strict teacher, and everyone on the retreat was being very quiet, moving slowly, and trying to be impeccably mindful. It was an intense time of training. At meal time, we would all enter the dining room silently and begin taking food, mindful of each movement.

One day, the person on line in front of me at the serving table lifted up the cover on a pot of food. As he put it down on the table, it suddenly dropped to the floor making a huge clanging noise. The very first thought that went through my mind was, "It wasn't me!" Now, where did that thought come from? With awareness, one can only smile at these uninvited guests in the mind.

Through the practice of meditation we begin to see the full range of the mind's activities: old unskillful patterns as well as wholesome thoughts and feelings. We learn to be with the whole passing show. As we become more accepting, a certain lightness develops

about it all. And the lighter and more accepting we become with ourselves, the lighter and
more accepting we are with others. We're not
so prone to judge the minds of others, once
we have carefully seen our own. The poet,
W.H. Auden, says it well: "Love your crooked
neighbor with all your crooked heart."

Spacious acceptance doesn't mean that we
act on everything equally. Awareness gives us
the option of *choosing wisely*: we can choose
which patterns should be developed and culti-
vated, and which should be abandoned.

Just as the focused lens of a microscope
enables us to see hidden levels of reality, so too
a concentrated mind opens us to deeper levels
of experience and more subtle movements of
thought and emotion. Without this power of
concentration, we stay on the surface of things.

If we are committed to deepening our understanding, we need to practice mindfulness and
gradually strengthen concentration.

One of the gifts of the teachings is the
reminder that we can do this—each and every
one of us.

PRACTICING IN DAILY LIFE

In our busy lives in this complex and often con-
fusing world, what practical steps can we take
to train our minds?

The first step is to establish a regular, daily
meditation practice. This takes discipline. It's
not always easy to set aside time each day for
meditation; so many other things call to us. But
as with any training, if we practice regularly we
begin to enjoy the fruits. Of course, not every
sitting will be concentrated. Sometimes we'll be

feeling bored or restless. These are the inevitable ups and downs of practice. It's the commitment and regularity of practice that is important, not how any one sitting feels.

Pablo Casals, the world renowned cellist, still practiced three hours a day when he was ninety-three. When asked why he still practiced at that age, he said, "I'm beginning to see some improvement."

The training in meditation will only happen through your own effort. No one can do it for you. There are many techniques and traditions, and you can find the one most suitable for you. But regularity of practice is what effects a transformation. If we do it, it begins to happen; if we don't do it, we continue acting out the various patterns of our conditioning.

No one can do it for you.

The second step is to train ourselves in staying mindful and aware of the body throughout the day. As we go through our daily activities, we frequently get lost in thoughts of past and future, not staying grounded in the awareness of our bodies.

A simple, useful feedback to remind us when we're lost in thought is the very common feeling of *rushing*. Rushing is a feeling of toppling forward. Our minds run ahead of us, focusing on where we want to go, instead of settling into our bodies where we are.

Learn to pay attention to this feeling of rushing—which does not particularly have to do with how fast we are going. We can feel rushed

while moving slowly, and we can be moving
quickly and still be settled in our bodies.

The feeling of rushing simply reminds us
that we're not present. If you can, notice what
thought or emotion has captured the attention.
Then, just for a moment, stop and settle back
into the body: feel the foot on the ground, feel
the next step.

**A little while alone in your room will
prove more valuable than anything else
that could ever be given you.**

RUMI

The Buddha made a very powerful statement
about this practice: "Mindfulness of the body

leads to nirvana." This is not a superficial practice. Mindfulness of the body keeps us present—
and therefore, we know what's going on. The
practice is difficult to remember, but not difficult to do. It's all in the training: sitting regularly
and being mindful of the body during the day.

To develop deeper concentration and mindfulness, to be more present in our bodies, and
to have a skillful relationship with thoughts and
emotions, we need not only daily training, but
also time for retreat. It's very helpful, at times,
to disengage from the busyness of our lives, for
intensive spiritual practice.

Retreat time is not a luxury. If we are genuinely and deeply committed to awakening, to
freedom—to whatever words express the highest value you hold—a retreat is an essential part
of the path.

We need to create a rhythm in our lives, establishing a balance between times when we are engaged, active, and relating in the world and times when we turn inward. The great Sufi poet Rumi very aptly noted, "A little while alone in your room will prove more valuable than anything else that could ever be given you."

At first this "going inside" could be for a day, a weekend, or a week. At our meditation center, we also offer a three-month retreat every year; and at the new Forest Refuge, people have come for as long as a year. We can do whatever feels appropriate and possible to find balanced rhythm between our lives in the world and the inner silence of a retreat. In this way we develop concentration and mindfulness on deeper and deeper levels, which then makes it possible to be in the world in a more loving and compassionate way.

THE LIGHT OF WISDOM

The first field of training is morality and the refinement of true inner beauty. The second is developing concentration and mindful aware-ness. The third field of training is wisdom. We cultivate this both through specific meditative practices and through wise attention in our lives. By just paying attention, a transforming wisdom becomes available to us.

Times of difficulty present us with a rich, but commonly overlooked, source of wisdom. When we're going through some period of suf-fering—if we are sufficiently motivated to look carefully—we can learn much about the nature of suffering and the nature of freedom.

In difficult times, we often tend to look out-
ward with blame and judgment, or we look
inward with self-blame and self-judgment.
Instead, we could let go of the judgments and
take an interest in the suffering itself. What is
causing it? What forces are at work in our
mind? Is there attachment, possessiveness, fear,
or expectation?

Don't side with yourself.

BANKEI

Some time ago, I was involved in a highly
charged organizational conflict. It seemed so
obvious to me that I was seeing the situation
clearly. Of course, people with opposing views

thought the same thing. Communications were getting very heated, with feelings of anger and defensiveness running high. At a certain point, feeling my own suffering and that of others, I stepped back and asked myself a question that proved very freeing: "Why do the others feel the way they do?" As soon as I was no longer caught in judging and blaming, it was easier to understand other people's strong feelings and points of view. As Bankei, a seventeenth-century Zen master, reminds us: "Don't side with yourself."

Life provides us with on-going opportunities to understand the Buddha's Noble Truths: suffering, its cause, its end, and the path to this freeing of the heart and mind.

THE PRACTICE OF REFLECTING ON IMPERMANENCE

We also develop wisdom through a very clear seeing and recollection of impermanence, and through the recollection of death. These are powerful teachings. We can understand imper-manence on so many levels, from the birth and death of galaxies to the fleeting change of mind moments.

Walking in the New England woods, one often comes upon old stone walls and crum-bling foundations of houses, and it brings to mind the many life stories and histories that must have happened on that land—all come and gone over the centuries. Reflection on impermanence leads us to a very important and demanding question. When we experience the truth of impermanence, not just as a concept, but as a genuinely felt insight, we are forced to ask, "What is truly of value?" Are we valuing things that are simply going to pass away? Or is there something else, something greater?

It helps me to imagine myself on my deathbed. I feel myself dying, and then, looking back from that vantage point, I think: What would I have wanted to accomplish in my life? How would I have wanted to live? This reflection provides a powerful perspective.

The real voyage of discovery consists not in seeing new landscapes, but in having new eyes.

MARCEL PROUST

Without this perspective, life often seems to unfold without any particular direction. We are buffeted by circumstances and living in the inertia of our habitual conditioning—and, then, one day it's over. We do not need to live and die that way, but we do need to be clear about our values and about what human great-ness we might accomplish.

The secret is to ask these questions now, before our deaths, in order to clarify our sense of purpose and meaning. We will then make more appropriate choices, because we see what is of value and what is not. We are artists, and life, itself, is our medium.

UNDERSTANDING SELFLESSNESS

Wisdom comes from a deep understanding of

impermanence. It also develops through a greater and greater experience of selflessness, of moving beyond our very small world of ego identification. In a surprising way, mindfulness and investigation of thoughts and emotions deepen our understanding of selflessness. There is a momentous difference between being lost in or identified with a thought or emotion, and the spaciousness of a mind that simply sees them arise and pass away in the open sky of awareness.

One Tibetan text says, "Thoughts that wander through our minds have no roots, no home." But with most thoughts that come through our minds we do feel, "This is mine. This is who I am."

Emotions, too, simply arise out of conditions and pass away as conditions change, like clouds forming and dissolving in the clear, open sky. Although emotions are what we most often personalize, taking them to be "I" or "mine" is a spiritual knot: the place where we contract into a small sense of self.

When you recognize the selfless nature of phenomena, the energy to bring about the good of others dawns uncontrived and effortless.

On the deepest level, we become mindful of consciousness itself. On this subtle level, we learn not to identify even with awareness, cut-ting though any sense of this knowing faculty as being "I" or "mine." As the Buddha said to

his son, Rahula, "You should consider all phenomena with proper wisdom: 'This is not
mine, this is not I, this is not myself.'"

To cultivate this radical transformation of
understanding, I've found it useful in meditation to reframe experience in the passive
voice: for example, "the breath being known,"
"sensations being known," "thoughts being
known." This language construction takes the
"I" out of the picture and opens us to the
probing question, "Known by what?" This
question can then lead us to experience directly—moment after moment—the unfolding
mystery of awareness.

Through the growing realization of selflessness, we develop a deepening sense of connec-
tion. We no longer need to strive for—or rely

on—particular forms of relationship to feel connected, because there is no longer anyone there to be separate. As one teaching points out, "When you recognize the selfless nature of phenomena, the energy to bring about the good of others dawns uncontrived and effortless." Wisdom and love become one.

At different times in our lives, we may get glimpses of something beyond our ordinary, conventional reality, touching a space that transforms our vision of who we are and what the world is. Just as the light of a single candle can dispel the darkness of a thousand years, the moment we light a single candle of wisdom, no matter how long or deep our confusion, igno-rance is dispelled.

Come and see; look deeply at your own life
and see for yourself. This is the real nature of
the spiritual journey.

About the Author

JOSEPH GOLDSTEIN is a cofounder of the Insight Meditation Society in Barre, Massachusetts, where he is one of the resident guiding teachers. He is the author of *One Dharma: The Emerging Western Buddhism; Insight Meditation: The Practice of Freedom, Seeking the Heart of Wisdom;* and *The Experience of Insight.* He lectures and leads retreats around the world.

For information about the teachings and retreat offerings, please contact Insight Meditation Society, 1230 Pleasant St., Barre, MA 01005 or visit the website at www.dharma.org.

·   *About Wisdom Publications*   ·

WISDOM PUBLICATIONS, a nonprofit publisher,
is dedicated to making available authentic works
relating to Buddhism for the benefit of all. We publish
books by ancient and modern masters in all traditions
of Buddhism, translations of important texts, and origi-
nal scholarship. Additionally, we offer books that explore
East-West themes unfolding as traditional Buddhism
encounters our modern culture in all its aspects. Our
titles are published with the appreciation of Buddhism
as a living philosophy, and with the special commitment
to preserve and transmit important works from Buddhism's many traditions.

To learn more about Wisdom, or to browse books
online, visit our website at www.wisdompubs.org.

You may request a copy of our catalog online or by
writing to this address:

Wisdom Publications
199 Elm Street
Somerville, Massachusetts 02144 USA
Telephone: 617-776-7416 ● Fax: 617-776-7841
Email: info@wisdompubs.org
www.wisdompubs.org

THE WISDOM TRUST

As a nonprofit publisher, Wisdom is dedicated to the publication of Dharma books for the benefit of all sentient beings and dependent upon the kindness and generosity of sponsors in order to do so. If you would like to make a donation to Wisdom, you may do so through our website or our Somerville office. If you would like to help sponsor the publication of a book, please write or email us at the address above.

Thank you.

Wisdom is a nonprofit, charitable 501(c)(3) organization affiliated with the Foundation for the Preservation of the Mahayana Tradition (FPMT).